# GAME CHANGERS

## 400 Momentum Shifters for the Game of Life

Written and Compiled by
Bruce Hamsher

Toward the Goal Ministries Inc.
508 Luzern St.
Sugarcreek, OH 44681
330-231-7277
bruce@towardthegoal.net
www.towardthegoal.net

Publishing History
First Printing, January 2016

ISBN 978-0-692-61391-7

Designed and Printed by:
Newhouse Printing Company
111 N. Walnut St.
Dover, OH 44622
www.newhouseprinting.com

Printed in the United States of America

Bruce Hamsher resides in Sugarcreek, Ohio, with
his wife, Jocelyn, and sons, Micah, Ty and Cade.
He is the Founder/CEO of Toward the Goal Ministries
Inc., and also enjoys his role as Leadership Coach at ProVia.
His passion is to see and help people grow into their full,
God-given potential.

## Thanks...

*To Jocelyn for sharing life together and for becoming
the best "Game Changer" I know.*

*To Micah, Ty and Cade…these words are really for you.
You are the best of the best.*

*To The King of all Game Changers –
"…Through the obedience of Christ,
many are made righteous."
(Romans 5:19b)*

# CONTENTS

# GAME CHANGERS

*"Let the wise listen and add to their learning and let the discerning get guidance." Proverbs 1:5*

Over the years in my various leadership positions of coaching, mentoring, pastoring, counseling and parenting, I have had the privilege of facilitating and participating in many leadership learning initiatives. I've done my best to add to my learning and to get guidance as the above proverb states by utilizing my two ears and one mouth in that ratio. If you know me, you know that's hard for me sometimes, but I've tried.

As I've listened to many people, I've also collected a lot of chicken scratch notes and have quickly jotted down thoughts and ideas which would pop into my head while reading or engaging in a great conversation.

This resource contains a compilation of these impromptu jottings as well as some truths I've known and taught for years. I've given the title of "Game Changers" to this collection because that is what they've become to me and countless others. Whether they've brought about clarity, touched on a next level nerve or simply changed the momentum of the final outcome, many of them continue to help change the way we look at ourselves and the people in our spheres of influence.

I must say that I do not claim authorship of all the content. While some of these writings are original with me, others are a form of someone else's idea or thought process, often drawn out from a group discussion. Regardless, they collectively mirror the truth found in Romans 12:2 which says, "…Let God transform you into a new person by changing the way you think." It's true, when I think differently, I act differently. And ultimately, my actions become the words to my life's story.

Start a **Game Changers Study Group** in order to learn together and to get the most depth out of the content. This works best by covering one section of "Game Changers" per session.

"Game Changers" is perfect for:
- Leadership groups in the workplace
- Coffee shop study groups
- One-on-one Coaching
- Small groups at school or church
- Staff development
- Family discussion starters

**Book of Proverbs Reading Plan** In scripture, Proverbs contains 31 chapters. Recognize the day of the month and read the corresponding section. You will become wiser!

# SECTION 1

The more it's not about you,
the more you'll love what you do.

1. **Whatever you feed grows, whatever you starve dies.**
   *What does this say to me?*

   *How could I apply this to my life?*

2. **With negative reactions…it's not personal, it's positional.**
   *What does this say to me?*

   *How could I apply this to my life?*

3. **You'll most likely find what you're looking for.**
   *What does this say to me?*

   *How could I apply this to my life?*

4. **When the student is ready, the teacher appears.**
   *What does this say to me?*

   *How could I apply this to my life?*

5. **Just because you can, doesn't mean you should.**
   *What does this say to me?*

   *How could I apply this to my life?*

6. **It seems easier to control people than to love them.**
   *What does this say to me?*

   *How could I apply this to my life?*

7. **Say no to good things, so you can say yes to the best things.**
   *What does this say to me?*

   *How could I apply this to my life?*

8. **Slow cookers make the tastiest food.**
   *What does this say to me?*

   *How could I apply this to my life?*

9. **It's more the Who than the Do.**
   *What does this say to me?*

   *How could I apply this to my life?*

10. **The best way to become a stronger person is to continually lift people up.**
    *What does this say to me?*

    *How could I apply this to my life?*

11. **Ownership includes taxes and leadership includes sacrifice.**
    *What does this say to me?*

    *How could I apply this to my life?*

12. **Sweeping things under the rug eventually ruins the floor.**
    *What does this say to me?*

    *How could I apply this to my life?*

13. **However you act is an invitation for others around you to do the same.**
    *What does this say to me?*

    *How could I apply this to my life?*

14. **In a traffic jam, I'm taking up the same amount of space as everyone else.**
    *What does this say to me?*

    *How could I apply this to my life?*

15. **Twelve pieces of pie and people stay hungry, four pieces and there's more than enough.**
    *What does this say to me?*

    *How could I apply this to my life?*

16. **Our actions often speak so loud that people can't hear what we're saying.**
    *What does this say to me?*

    *How could I apply this to my life?*

17. **When people do right, nothing is said; when people do wrong, everything is said.**
    *What does this say to me?*

    *How could I apply this to my life?*

18. **That which gets recognized gets repeated.**
    *What does this say to me?*

    *How could I apply this to my life?*

19. **Don't talk about someone, do something for them.**
    *What does this say to me?*

    *How could I apply this to my life?*

20. **Without tests, we're unsure how to measure our progress.**
    *What does this say to me?*

    *How could I apply this to my life?*

21. **The more it's not about you, the more you'll love what you do.**
    *What does this say to me?*

    *How could I apply this to my life?*

22. **You wouldn't be so concerned what people think of you, if you only knew how little they do.**
    *What does this say to me?*

    *How could I apply this to my life?*

23. **Never give wordy evidence of the fact that you really have nothing to say.**
    *What does this say to me?*

    *How could I apply this to my life?*

24. **Calm is contagious.**
    *What does this say to me?*

    *How could I apply this to my life?*

25. **The visibles are what we see; the invisibles are what really matter.**
    *What does this say to me?*

    *How could I apply this to my life?*

# SECTION 2

Motivation happens best by extending
trust, not fear.

**26.** **As you rise above the clouds, the sun shines bright.**
*What does this say to me?*

*How could I apply this to my life?*

**27.** **You don't have to rebuild what you haven't destroyed.**
*What does this say to me?*

*How could I apply this to my life?*

**28.** **Dependable people are like oxygen to the soul.**
*What does this say to me?*

*How could I apply this to my life?*

**29.** **Talk positive about others when they're not around to hear it.**
*What does this say to me?*

*How could I apply this to my life?*

**30.** **Tend to the garden of another and your crop will overflow.**
*What does this say to me?*

*How could I apply this to my life?*

**31.** **Proper perspective changes everything.**
*What does this say to me?*

*How could I apply this to my life?*

**32.** **Settling for easy is as unhealthy as a steady diet of junk food.**
*What does this say to me?*

*How could I apply this to my life?*

33. **More Investment = More Interest = More Influence.**
*What does this say to me?*


*How could I apply this to my life?*


34. **When an improper motive is discovered, trust is destroyed.**
*What does this say to me?*


*How could I apply this to my life?*


35. **Be the kind of worker you would want to work with.**
*What does this say to me?*


*How could I apply this to my life?*


36. **A wise person has character while a shrewd person is a character.**
*What does this say to me?*


*How could I apply this to my life?*


37. **I become more valuable to my team as I become more versatile with my contributions.**
*What does this say to me?*


*How could I apply this to my life?*


38. **Refresh others and life will begin to make sense.**
*What does this say to me?*


*How could I apply this to my life?*

39. **When trust increases, confusion decreases; when trust decreases, frustration increases.**
*What does this say to me?*

*How could I apply this to my life?*

40. **Motivation happens best by extending trust, not fear.**
*What does this say to me?*

*How could I apply this to my life?*

41. **Be careful not to confuse activity with productivity.**
*What does this say to me?*

*How could I apply this to my life?*

42. **Emotional preparation precedes effective conversation.**
*What does this say to me?*

*How could I apply this to my life?*

43. **Present solutions to other person's problems as if they were your own.**
*What does this say to me?*

*How could I apply this to my life?*

44. **If a "weather report" is required before others approach you, anxiety will rule them.**
*What does this say to me?*

*How could I apply this to my life?*

45. **Proactive people look ahead and anticipate the future.**
*What does this say to me?*

*How could I apply this to my life?*

46. **Reactive people respond to events only after the problems arise.**
*What does this say to me?*

*How could I apply this to my life?*

47. **Today's complacency becomes tomorrow's captivity.**
*What does this say to me?*

*How could I apply this to my life?*

48. **When the competition becomes internal, the ship begins to sink.**
*What does this say to me?*

*How could I apply this to my life?*

49. **It's nearly impossible to be thankful and stressful at the same time.**
*What does this say to me?*

*How could I apply this to my life?*

50. **The most satisfied people look for work at work and look for life in life.**
*What does this say to me?*

*How could I apply this to my life?*

# SECTION 3

A truth becomes part of one's past;
a lie becomes part of one's future.

**51.** See problems as they could be improved, not as they presently are.

*What does this say to me?*


*How could I apply this to my life?*


**52.** Dirty dishes mean your belly is full.

*What does this say to me?*


*How could I apply this to my life?*


**53.** Interruptions often provide us with our best opportunities.

*What does this say to me?*


*How could I apply this to my life?*


**54.** One way to do more is to do less.

*What does this say to me?*


*How could I apply this to my life?*


**55.** A controlled river is productive, an uncontrolled flood is destructive.

*What does this say to me?*


*How could I apply this to my life?*


**56.** To the measure that I guard my lips, I guard my life.

*What does this say to me?*


*How could I apply this to my life?*


**57.** Verbally communicating everything which races to one's mind lacks wisdom.

*What does this say to me?*


*How could I apply this to my life?*

58. **Words either build up or tear down.**
*What does this say to me?*

*How could I apply this to my life?*

59. **I'm either a burden or a blessing.**
*What does this say to me?*

*How could I apply this to my life?*

60. **Get the best out of the opportunity at hand instead of trying to get out of the opportunity at hand.**
*What does this say to me?*

*How could I apply this to my life?*

61. **Mindless routines tend to dull the blade.**
*What does this say to me?*

*How could I apply this to my life?*

62. **You are the owner of your actions and reputation.**
*What does this say to me?*

*How could I apply this to my life?*

63. **When honesty is not honored, everyone is affected.**
*What does this say to me?*

*How could I apply this to my life?*

64. **A truth becomes part of one's past; a lie becomes part of one's future.**
*What does this say to me?*

*How could I apply this to my life?*

**65.** **Honesty is relaying the facts while leaving the right impression.**
*What does this say to me?*

*How could I apply this to my life?*


**66.** **A temperature of 98.6 is optimum; 93.6 and 103.6 bring about the same concerns.**
*What does this say to me?*

*How could I apply this to my life?*


**67.** **It can be very embarrassing to be wrong at the top of your voice.**
*What does this say to me?*

*How could I apply this to my life?*


**68.** **Ships were built to sail, not to stay safe in the harbor.**
*What does this say to me?*

*How could I apply this to my life?*


**69.** **Don't mistake speed bumps for stop signs.**
*What does this say to me?*

*How could I apply this to my life?*


**70.** **The way you think determines the way you live and love.**
*What does this say to me?*

*How could I apply this to my life?*


**71.** **Slow with people is fast and fast with people is slow.**
*What does this say to me?*

*How could I apply this to my life?*

72. **When our emotions hijack the steering wheel, call the ambulance in advance.**
*What does this say to me?*

*How could I apply this to my life?*

73. **The one who serves first is the leader.**
*What does this say to me?*

*How could I apply this to my life?*

74. **Lead like you parent.**
*What does this say to me?*

*How could I apply this to my life?*

75. **The person closest to the problem, often has the best solution.**
*What does this say to me?*

*How could I apply this to my life?*

# SECTION 4

Contentment is found in wanting
what I already have.

76. **You don't have to if you get to.**

*What does this say to me?*


*How could I apply this to my life?*


77. **We either work to make a paycheck or to make a difference.**

*What does this say to me?*


*How could I apply this to my life?*


78. **Watch as I handle compliments and you will know the real me.**

*What does this say to me?*


*How could I apply this to my life?*


79. **The best leaders in life are the best students of life.**

*What does this say to me?*


*How could I apply this to my life?*


80. **People will never forget how you made them feel.**

*What does this say to me?*


*How could I apply this to my life?*


81. **Love cannot be commanded or demanded, only given.**

*What does this say to me?*


*How could I apply this to my life?*


82. **Progress always involves pressure, courage and risk.**

*What does this say to me?*


*How could I apply this to my life?*

83. **Whine and complain and people will line up to form a choir.**
*What does this say to me?*

*How could I apply this to my life?*

84. **Contentment is found in wanting what I already have.**
*What does this say to me?*

*How could I apply this to my life?*

85. **Our greatest fear is found in succeeding in things that don't really matter.**
*What does this say to me?*

*How could I apply this to my life?*

86. **T-I-M-E – This Is My Example.**
*What does this say to me?*

*How could I apply this to my life?*

87. **There is a God, and He's not me.**
*What does this say to me?*

*How could I apply this to my life?*

88. **Adversity is the best teacher.**
*What does this say to me?*

*How could I apply this to my life?*

89. **Visit your past, just don't live there.**
*What does this say to me?*

*How could I apply this to my life?*

**90.** **Gratitude is the one answer to the many problems we face.**
*What does this say to me?*

*How could I apply this to my life?*

**91.** **Stressed spelled backwards is desserts.**
*What does this say to me?*

*How could I apply this to my life?*

**92.** **Don't wait for the funeral; give your bouquets to the living.**
*What does this say to me?*

*How could I apply this to my life?*

**93.** **My actions reveal my truest intentions.**
*What does this say to me?*

*How could I apply this to my life?*

**94.** **Ask five questions for every one statement you make.**
*What does this say to me?*

*How could I apply this to my life?*

**95.** **You can't steer a parked car.**
*What does this say to me?*

*How could I apply this to my life?*

**96.** **Whatever you focus on expands.**
*What does this say to me?*

*How could I apply this to my life?*

97. **Reconciliation is more important than being right.**

*What does this say to me?*

*How could I apply this to my life?*

98. **Without wood a fire goes out.**

*What does this say to me?*

*How could I apply this to my life?*

99. **Fear and pride feed unhealthy conflict.**

*What does this say to me?*

*How could I apply this to my life?*

100. **Clarity and understanding feed healthy conflict.**

*What does this say to me?*

*How could I apply this to my life?*

# SECTION 5

Truly get to know someone and you'll be more compassionate and less critical.

**101. Criticism shouldn't bother us if we're committed to the truth.**
*What does this say to me?*

*How could I apply this to my life?*

**102. Praise others in public, correct others in private.**
*What does this say to me?*

*How could I apply this to my life?*

**103. Getting loud is generally a sign of insecurity.**
*What does this say to me?*

*How could I apply this to my life?*

**104. Influence begins when you ask people questions about things they like to talk about.**
*What does this say to me?*

*How could I apply this to my life?*

**105. Truly get to know someone and you'll be more compassionate and less critical.**
*What does this say to me?*

*How could I apply this to my life?*

**106. Freedom is enjoyed best within established boundaries.**
*What does this say to me?*

*How could I apply this to my life?*

107. **Narrow, difficult roads often lead to the most beautiful views.**

*What does this say to me?*

*How could I apply this to my life?*

108. **Either you will lead your life or life will lead you.**

*What does this say to me?*

*How could I apply this to my life?*

109. **A complaining lifestyle leads to a complicated life.**

*What does this say to me?*

*How could I apply this to my life?*

110. **No medal is awarded for starting out in first place.**

*What does this say to me?*

*How could I apply this to my life?*

111. **The more we fear failure, the more we attract failure.**

*What does this say to me?*

*How could I apply this to my life?*

112. **Dishonesty happens in private and is revealed in public.**

*What does this say to me?*

*How could I apply this to my life?*

113. **You are living in the house you've built.**

*What does this say to me?*

*How could I apply this to my life?*

**114.** **How we think is what we become.**

*What does this say to me?*

*How could I apply this to my life?*

**115.** **The truth has a way of setting one free.**

*What does this say to me?*

*How could I apply this to my life?*

**116.** **Spectators are experts in their own mind.**

*What does this say to me?*

*How could I apply this to my life?*

**117.** **It's difficult to give direction to a falling tree.**

*What does this say to me?*

*How could I apply this to my life?*

**118.** **We're either bringing about clarity or confusion.**

*What does this say to me?*

*How could I apply this to my life?*

**119.** **Courage is fear that has said its prayers.**

*What does this say to me?*

*How could I apply this to my life?*

**120.** **Great intentions have made no person famous.**

*What does this say to me?*

*How could I apply this to my life?*

121. **I trust you only to the extent that I trust myself.**

*What does this say to me?*

*How could I apply this to my life?*

122. **Attitude and effort are more important than results.**

*What does this say to me?*

*How could I apply this to my life?*

123. **Attack the issue, not the person.**

*What does this say to me?*

*How could I apply this to my life?*

124. **Be ready and willing to work yourself out of your job.**

*What does this say to me?*

*How could I apply this to my life?*

125. **Our future disappears when we're obsessed with our past.**

*What does this say to me?*

*How could I apply this to my life?*

# SECTION 6

What I learn in training is greater than
the gold medal.

126. **Given enough time, the smoke will clear.**

*What does this say to me?*


*How could I apply this to my life?*


127. **Listen to what isn't being said and the truth will appear.**

*What does this say to me?*


*How could I apply this to my life?*


128. **Insecure people ask their own questions and quickly answer them.**

*What does this say to me?*


*How could I apply this to my life?*


129. **Fear almost always precedes courage.**

*What does this say to me?*


*How could I apply this to my life?*


130. **Check the mirror first then look out the window.**

*What does this say to me?*


*How could I apply this to my life?*


131. **You begin to see yourself the way I see you.**

*What does this say to me?*


*How could I apply this to my life?*


132. **I am not responsible for your response, only for my actions.**

*What does this say to me?*


*How could I apply this to my life?*

**133.** What I learn in training is greater than the gold medal.

*What does this say to me?*

*How could I apply this to my life?*

**134.** Clarity and Consistency will get the job done every time.

*What does this say to me?*

*How could I apply this to my life?*

**135.** When the line is crossed, the story changes.

*What does this say to me?*

*How could I apply this to my life?*

**136.** A critical spirit puts the brakes on creativity.

*What does this say to me?*

*How could I apply this to my life?*

**137.** Many traditions are void of common sense.

*What does this say to me?*

*How could I apply this to my life?*

**138.** We have two ears and one mouth for good reason.

*What does this say to me?*

*How could I apply this to my life?*

**139.** If I'm forever casting doubt, I'm struggling to find my own happiness.

*What does this say to me?*

*How could I apply this to my life?*

140. **The truth does not cease to exist because it is ignored.**
*What does this say to me?*

*How could I apply this to my life?*

141. **Controlling our emotions is healthy, hiding them is detrimental.**
*What does this say to me?*

*How could I apply this to my life?*

142. **Our calendars and our checkbooks expose our priorities.**
*What does this say to me?*

*How could I apply this to my life?*

143. **By default, I will often repeat what was modeled for me.**
*What does this say to me?*

*How could I apply this to my life?*

144. **A few wise people make the best decisions for the masses.**
*What does this say to me?*

*How could I apply this to my life?*

145. **Hoarders never have enough. Givers always have more than enough.**
*What does this say to me?*

*How could I apply this to my life?*

146. **Paralysis by analysis keeps the future invisible.**
*What does this say to me?*

*How could I apply this to my life?*

147. **If you don't have enough money, the solution is not to borrow more.**
*What does this say to me?*

*How could I apply this to my life?*

148. **Failure or success does not happen overnight.**
*What does this say to me?*

*How could I apply this to my life?*

149. **In sports and in life, without a goal, confusion and chaos wins the game.**
*What does this say to me?*

*How could I apply this to my life?*

150. **Things accomplished with little effort are seldom sustainable.**
*What does this say to me?*

*How could I apply this to my life?*

# SECTION 7

Move toward your problems and face them
or they will chase after you
the rest of your life.

151. **Move toward your problems and face them or they will chase after you the rest of your life.**
*What does this say to me?*

*How could I apply this to my life?*

152. **Make sure your goals weren't set by someone else.**
*What does this say to me?*

*How could I apply this to my life?*

153. **When nothing's at stake, the game is a yawner.**
*What does this say to me?*

*How could I apply this to my life?*

154. **We should help people out, not help them stay in.**
*What does this say to me?*

*How could I apply this to my life?*

155. **Hasty shortcuts will eventually lengthen your trip.**
*What does this say to me?*

*How could I apply this to my life?*

156. **Embrace the ups and downs of life, flat-lining means you're dead.**
*What does this say to me?*

*How could I apply this to my life?*

157. **Plan your week at 80% full and you'll get more done.**
*What does this say to me?*

*How could I apply this to my life?*

158. **I must first lead myself before I can lead others.**
*What does this say to me?*

*How could I apply this to my life?*

159. **Whatever I do first begins as a thought.**
*What does this say to me?*

*How could I apply this to my life?*

160. **We live our lives with reward or regret.**
*What does this say to me?*

*How could I apply this to my life?*

161. **The more we give, the richer we become.**
*What does this say to me?*

*How could I apply this to my life?*

162. **Words without actions are like offering a menu with no food.**
*What does this say to me?*

*How could I apply this to my life?*

163. **Become a producer, not just a consumer.**
*What does this say to me?*

*How could I apply this to my life?*

164. **My internal customers are my family, friends and co-workers.**
*What does this say to me?*

*How could I apply this to my life?*

**165.** Very few people quit companies, most quit their bosses.

*What does this say to me?*

*How could I apply this to my life?*

**166.** Choose truth over emotion, the outcome depends on it.

*What does this say to me?*

*How could I apply this to my life?*

**167.** We are responsible to people, not for people.

*What does this say to me?*

*How could I apply this to my life?*

**168.** A high character amateur can be more valuable than a highly skilled know-it-all.

*What does this say to me?*

*How could I apply this to my life?*

**169.** Never become so important that you can't be replaced.

*What does this say to me?*

*How could I apply this to my life?*

**170.** With people...Recognize their passion, Reveal their potential and Reward their progress.

*What does this say to me?*

*How could I apply this to my life?*

171. **My life provides an excuse or an example.**

   *What does this say to me?*

   *How could I apply this to my life?*

172. **Opportunities are abundant for those who want them.**

   *What does this say to me?*

   *How could I apply this to my life?*

173. **Ambition is the third baseman diving after the foul ball.**

   *What does this say to me?*

   *How could I apply this to my life?*

174. **Owning another person's decision or behavior could prove costly to everyone involved.**

   *What does this say to me?*

   *How could I apply this to my life?*

175. **Wise people will give things as a gift, asking nothing in return.**

   *What does this say to me?*

   *How could I apply this to my life?*

# SECTION 8

We often yell the loudest when giving
the silent treatment.

176. **When we see things only through our lens, judgment wins the race.**
*What does this say to me?*

*How could I apply this to my life?*

177. **When we understand people at their core, grace and mercy have a chance to appear.**
*What does this say to me?*

*How could I apply this to my life?*

178. **Whether an idea, action or property...if you don't own it, you won't take good care of it and it will lose its value.**
*What does this say to me?*

*How could I apply this to my life?*

179. **Although your name may not be on the sign, you are the owner of your work.**
*What does this say to me?*

*How could I apply this to my life?*

180. **You can rent a tool, house or an apartment, but you can't rent a friendship with much success.**
*What does this say to me?*

*How could I apply this to my life?*

181. **My inability to forgive traps me and keeps me held to my past.**
*What does this say to me?*

*How could I apply this to my life?*

182. **Feelings buried alive never die.**

*What does this say to me?*

*How could I apply this to my life?*

183. **Listen to understand before speaking to be understood.**

*What does this say to me?*

*How could I apply this to my life?*

184. **Most people who are always busy are not facing their deeper issues.**

*What does this say to me?*

*How could I apply this to my life?*

185. **We often yell the loudest when giving someone the silent treatment.**

*What does this say to me?*

*How could I apply this to my life?*

186. **We tend to condemn what we don't do and justify the rest.**

*What does this say to me?*

*How could I apply this to my life?*

187. **Anger is an emotional response which causes many physical problems.**

*What does this say to me?*

*How could I apply this to my life?*

188. **Vulnerability equals strength.**

*What does this say to me?*

*How could I apply this to my life?*

**189.** If you look closer, obstacles often present new opportunities.
*What does this say to me?*

*How could I apply this to my life?*

**190.** You become known for what you give, not what you gain.
*What does this say to me?*

*How could I apply this to my life?*

**191.** Find out what people are doing right and let them know about it.
*What does this say to me?*

*How could I apply this to my life?*

**192.** We're either holding people down or lifting people up.
*What does this say to me?*

*How could I apply this to my life?*

**193.** Comparisons happen when I want what you already have.
*What does this say to me?*

*How could I apply this to my life?*

**194.** A decision convinces through words, a commitment convinces through proof.
*What does this say to me?*

*How could I apply this to my life?*

195. **People uptight with smokers and drinkers seem to have little problem with gluttony and gossip.**
*What does this say to me?*

*How could I apply this to my life?*

196. **The best leaders appear to be more collective then directive.**
*What does this say to me?*

*How could I apply this to my life?*

197. **Either I will stop it or it will stop me.**
*What does this say to me?*

*How could I apply this to my life?*

198. **Growth occurs when we live our lives by commitments rather than feelings.**
*What does this say to me?*

*How could I apply this to my life?*

199. **Make sure your video matches your audio.**
*What does this say to me?*

*How could I apply this to my life?*

200. **Hurting people hurt people and healed people heal people.**
*What does this say to me?*

*How could I apply this to my life?*

# SECTION 9

Great people are always the first in line to celebrate someone else's success.

201. **You can learn something from every person you meet...even if it's what not to do.**
*What does this say to me?*

*How could I apply this to my life?*

202. **If you have a problem with everyone and everything, you are the problem.**
*What does this say to me?*

*How could I apply this to my life?*

203. **Great people are always the first in line to celebrate someone else's success.**
*What does this say to me?*

*How could I apply this to my life?*

204. **A victim mentality is comparable to a slow death.**
*What does this say to me?*

*How could I apply this to my life?*

205. **As creditors we expect payment; as debtors we expect sympathy.**
*What does this say to me?*

*How could I apply this to my life?*

206. **Being quick to acknowledge others' mistakes will flatten your tire of influence.**
*What does this say to me?*

*How could I apply this to my life?*

**207.** Pressure is productive if we're properly prepared.

*What does this say to me?*

*How could I apply this to my life?*

**208.** Adapting to change is the key factor that will influence success.

*What does this say to me?*

*How could I apply this to my life?*

**209.** When I'm no longer teachable, I might as well pack it in.

*What does this say to me?*

*How could I apply this to my life?*

**210.** Organizing and attending a meeting means nothing unless a commitment to action occurs.

*What does this say to me?*

*How could I apply this to my life?*

**211.** When leaders gossip, complain and pass the blame, their people will do the same.

*What does this say to me?*

*How could I apply this to my life?*

**212.** Offering to help where help isn't asked for usually backfires.

*What does this say to me?*

*How could I apply this to my life?*

**213. Agreement and respect are separate issues.**

*What does this say to me?*


*How could I apply this to my life?*


**214. Learn first then contribute with your words.**

*What does this say to me?*


*How could I apply this to my life?*


**215. Know your limitations and freely share them with others.**

*What does this say to me?*


*How could I apply this to my life?*


**216. There is no such thing as 110%.**

*What does this say to me?*


*How could I apply this to my life?*


**217. Disagreement does not equal rejection.**

*What does this say to me?*


*How could I apply this to my life?*


**218. Earthly accomplishments are temporary; Heavenly rewards last forever.**

*What does this say to me?*


*How could I apply this to my life?*


**219. Acknowledge your mistake yourself or listen as others acknowledge it for you.**

*What does this say to me?*


*How could I apply this to my life?*

220. **The greatest teams and organizations reload vs. rebuild.**
*What does this say to me?*

*How could I apply this to my life?*

221. **My decisions have a ripple effect, they never just affect me.**
*What does this say to me?*

*How could I apply this to my life?*

222. **Don't confuse a full schedule with a fulfilling life.**
*What does this say to me?*

*How could I apply this to my life?*

223. **Windshields are much larger than rear view mirrors.**
*What does this say to me?*

*How could I apply this to my life?*

224. **When a question arises, either trust or suspicion builds the bridge.**
*What does this say to me?*

*How could I apply this to my life?*

225. **Like water poured into sand, the words we say can never be taken back.**
*What does this say to me?*

*How could I apply this to my life?*

# SECTION 10

Stagnant farm ponds are ignored
while flowing mountain streams are enjoyed.

226. **Be humble, but confident.**
*What does this say to me?*

*How could I apply this to my life?*

227. **Reorganize your stumbling blocks into stepping stones.**
*What does this say to me?*

*How could I apply this to my life?*

228. **What we think about is what we often end up doing.**
*What does this say to me?*

*How could I apply this to my life?*

229. **When my talk is big my walk is usually small.**
*What does this say to me?*

*How could I apply this to my life?*

230. **I'm living well when I put my compassion into action.**
*What does this say to me?*

*How could I apply this to my life?*

231. **Small acts of follow-through are greater than large grandiose ideas.**
*What does this say to me?*

*How could I apply this to my life?*

232. **Making time for people for no apparent reason is often the best reason of all.**
*What does this say to me?*

*How could I apply this to my life?*

233. **Shutting off the noise of ourselves will benefit everyone involved.**
*What does this say to me?*

*How could I apply this to my life?*

234. **A life jacket is useless unless you wear it.**
*What does this say to me?*

*How could I apply this to my life?*

235. **Early on people feed us, later we feed ourselves, finally we feed others.**
*What does this say to me?*

*How could I apply this to my life?*

236. **Stagnant farm ponds are ignored while flowing mountain streams are enjoyed.**
*What does this say to me?*

*How could I apply this to my life?*

237. **It takes little effort to know about someone and much effort to truly know them.**
*What does this say to me?*

*How could I apply this to my life?*

238. **The 17 inches from our head to our heart often feels more like a mile.**
*What does this say to me?*

*How could I apply this to my life?*

239. **A selfish person is dismissed while a selfless person is respected.**
*What does this say to me?*

*How could I apply this to my life?*

240. **A generous person will be more concerned with why they give, not what they give.**
*What does this say to me?*

*How could I apply this to my life?*

241. **No one receives a wrapped gift only to store it away in the corner of a closet.**
*What does this say to me?*

*How could I apply this to my life?*

242. **The best learners are the best question askers.**
*What does this say to me?*

*How could I apply this to my life?*

243. **It takes many individual pieces of sand to form a beach.**
*What does this say to me?*

*How could I apply this to my life?*

244. **I make a living by what I get and make a life by what I give away.**
*What does this say to me?*

*How could I apply this to my life?*

**245.** Unless trust is established, shared vision will be unattainable.

*What does this say to me?*

*How could I apply this to my life?*

**246.** When you don't know what to do and are at the end of your rope, choose love.

*What does this say to me?*

*How could I apply this to my life?*

**247.** Choose your battles wisely and your voice will become clearer to the listener.

*What does this say to me?*

*How could I apply this to my life?*

**248.** A wise person shovels the pile while it is still small.

*What does this say to me?*

*How could I apply this to my life?*

**249.** Never win the argument and lose the relationship.

*What does this say to me?*

*How could I apply this to my life?*

**250.** Patience wins out when I anticipate your response before approaching the subject.

*What does this say to me?*

*How could I apply this to my life?*

# SECTION 11

Trying to fix another person is like
trying to live in an igloo on the beach.

**251.** The traffic light switches to yellow when a person aches for position.

*What does this say to me?*

*How could I apply this to my life?*

**252.** You will initially doubt what I say and will ultimately believe what I do.

*What does this say to me?*

*How could I apply this to my life?*

**253.** You can't give what you don't have.

*What does this say to me?*

*How could I apply this to my life?*

**254.** Harvesting corn in June or December will get you the same return on your investment.

*What does this say to me?*

*How could I apply this to my life?*

**255.** If we let it go too long, we'll have to work twice as hard to get the same result and will double the frustration.

*What does this say to me?*

*How could I apply this to my life?*

**256.** When there's not a lot to do, even less gets accomplished.

*What does this say to me?*

*How could I apply this to my life?*

**257.** Better to say one thing ten times, then ten things one time.

*What does this say to me?*

*How could I apply this to my life?*

**258.** The more the leftovers are reheated, the less eager I am to eat them.

*What does this say to me?*

*How could I apply this to my life?*

**259.** My bad reputation stays intact as long as my mouth keeps chattering.

*What does this say to me?*

*How could I apply this to my life?*

**260.** Trying to fix another person is like trying to live in an igloo on the beach.

*What does this say to me?*

*How could I apply this to my life?*

**261.** My accomplishments aren't as important to you as I thought you thought they were.

*What does this say to me?*

*How could I apply this to my life?*

**262.** I don't deserve the majority of the praise or the criticism you give me.

*What does this say to me?*

*How could I apply this to my life?*

263. In that specific moment, whoever I am with becomes the priority.
*What does this say to me?*

*How could I apply this to my life?*

264. No game has ever been won by staying in the huddle. No life has ever been lived well by playing it safe.
*What does this say to me?*

*How could I apply this to my life?*

265. I may be attracted to your personality but I am influenced by your character.
*What does this say to me?*

*How could I apply this to my life?*

266. Bad people are capable of doing very good things, for very bad reasons.
*What does this say to me?*

*How could I apply this to my life?*

267. Fire before you hire; quit before you start.
*What does this say to me?*

*How could I apply this to my life?*

268. Hard work doesn't make you nearly as tired as a negative attitude does.
*What does this say to me?*

*How could I apply this to my life?*

**269.** Little by little, piece by piece, the puzzle is slowly put together.
*What does this say to me?*

*How could I apply this to my life?*

**270.** My life shrinks or expands in proportion to my courage.
*What does this say to me?*

*How could I apply this to my life?*

**271.** Responsible people make a difference, not an excuse.
*What does this say to me?*

*How could I apply this to my life?*

**272.** When justifications outweigh accountability, problems never go away.
*What does this say to me?*

*How could I apply this to my life?*

**273.** Better to have a small part of something big, than a big part of something small.
*What does this say to me?*

*How could I apply this to my life?*

**274.** Leadership is the one thing a leader cannot delegate.
*What does this say to me?*

*How could I apply this to my life?*

**275.** Awareness is the first step in the healing process.
*What does this say to me?*

*How could I apply this to my life?*

# SECTION 12

Secure people strive for service,
insecure people strive for status.

276. **When offended, do the opposite of what you feel like doing.**
*What does this say to me?*

*How could I apply this to my life?*

277. **Running from an uncomfortable issue puts you further behind.**
*What does this say to me?*

*How could I apply this to my life?*

278. **Focus first on what is right, not who is right; what went wrong, not who went wrong.**
*What does this say to me?*

*How could I apply this to my life?*

279. **Envisioning success first will ultimately lead you to it.**
*What does this say to me?*

*How could I apply this to my life?*

280. **Arrogance is like a bad odor that clears the room.**
*What does this say to me?*

*How could I apply this to my life?*

281. **When there is nothing to lose, hide or prove there is also nothing to fear.**
*What does this say to me?*

*How could I apply this to my life?*

282. **Secure people strive for service, insecure people strive for status.**
*What does this say to me?*

*How could I apply this to my life?*

283. **Some people complain about the darkness while others light a match.**
*What does this say to me?*

*How could I apply this to my life?*

284. **Be slow to prescribe a pill before knowing the problem.**
*What does this say to me?*

*How could I apply this to my life?*

285. **It takes zero percent effort on our part for weeds to grow.**
*What does this say to me?*

*How could I apply this to my life?*

286. **My individual trophy is remembered by me, our championship is remembered by all.**
*What does this say to me?*

*How could I apply this to my life?*

287. **Your pathway of success was paved by someone else's sacrifice.**
*What does this say to me?*

*How could I apply this to my life?*

288. **When one candle shares its light with another, it doubles the brightness of the room.**
*What does this say to me?*

*How could I apply this to my life?*

**289.** When emotions override reality, intelligence disappears.

*What does this say to me?*

*How could I apply this to my life?*

**290.** When nothing is made into something, something bigger is being hidden.

*What does this say to me?*

*How could I apply this to my life?*

**291.** The danger in trying to change a person is becoming more like them in the process.

*What does this say to me?*

*How could I apply this to my life?*

**292.** When leaders stay silent, followers become anxious and insecure.

*What does this say to me?*

*How could I apply this to my life?*

**293.** Our days are spent either preparing the future or repairing the past.

*What does this say to me?*

*How could I apply this to my life?*

**294.** When something becomes convenient, it quickly loses its value.

*What does this say to me?*

*How could I apply this to my life?*

**295.** Continual praises affect our person like continual raises affect our pocket book.

*What does this say to me?*

*How could I apply this to my life?*

**296.** Relationships flourish when we simply give to others what they need.

*What does this say to me?*

*How could I apply this to my life?*

**297.** Success is more about the people in the seats than the project on the table.

*What does this say to me?*

*How could I apply this to my life?*

**298.** Do for one what you wish you could do for the world.

*What does this say to me?*

*How could I apply this to my life?*

**299.** He who angers you controls you.

*What does this say to me?*

*How could I apply this to my life?*

**300.** In prosperity our friends know us, in adversity we know our friends.

*What does this say to me?*

*How could I apply this to my life?*

# SECTION 13

A great way to get out of your misery is to help someone else get out of theirs.

**301.** Paying attention to the tension brings about insight and growth.
*What does this say to me?*

*How could I apply this to my life?*

**302.** Most problems are possibilities waiting to be discovered.
*What does this say to me?*

*How could I apply this to my life?*

**303.** Innovation and creativity are often birthed out of chaos.
*What does this say to me?*

*How could I apply this to my life?*

**304.** Live in such a way that the minister won't have to lie at your funeral.
*What does this say to me?*

*How could I apply this to my life?*

**305.** Simple doesn't necessarily mean easy.
*What does this say to me?*

*How could I apply this to my life?*

**306.** Enjoying something isn't a requirement of doing it.
*What does this say to me?*

*How could I apply this to my life?*

**307.** The more you try to evade an issue, the closer it moves toward you.
*What does this say to me?*

*How could I apply this to my life?*

**308.** **Growth energizes leaders and paralyzes managers.**

*What does this say to me?*

*How could I apply this to my life?*

**309.** **The purpose of pruning is to produce even more.**

*What does this say to me?*

*How could I apply this to my life?*

**310.** **In primitive societies people are found with no watches and plenty of time.**

*What does this say to me?*

*How could I apply this to my life?*

**311.** **If you don't have time to do it right the first time, you won't have time to do it over the second and third time.**

*What does this say to me?*

*How could I apply this to my life?*

**312.** **Scheduled deadlines are great accountability partners.**

*What does this say to me?*

*How could I apply this to my life?*

**313.** **Be ready before the opportunity presents itself.**

*What does this say to me?*

*How could I apply this to my life?*

314. **Own a problem that isn't yours and pay the taxes you can't afford.**
*What does this say to me?*

*How could I apply this to my life?*

315. **Don't point out a problem without also providing a solution.**
*What does this say to me?*

*How could I apply this to my life?*

316. **Something is not truly communicated until it is received and understood.**
*What does this say to me?*

*How could I apply this to my life?*

317. **Ministry is often birthed out of misery.**
*What does this say to me?*

*How could I apply this to my life?*

318. **The best listeners are the best leaders.**
*What does this say to me?*

*How could I apply this to my life?*

319. **If things come easy, you're probably not risking much.**
*What does this say to me?*

*How could I apply this to my life?*

320. **The challenges I face will produce breakdowns or breakthroughs.**
*What does this say to me?*

*How could I apply this to my life?*

321. **A great way to get out of your misery is to help someone else get out of theirs.**

*What does this say to me?*

*How could I apply this to my life?*

322. **It can be very deceiving when you defeat poor competition.**

*What does this say to me?*

*How could I apply this to my life?*

323. **Listen 80% of the time and talk 20% of the time.**

*What does this say to me?*

*How could I apply this to my life?*

324. **Selfishness ruins today's opportunities and doubles tomorrow's troubles.**

*What does this say to me?*

*How could I apply this to my life?*

325. **Have a plan, but write it in pencil.**

*What does this say to me?*

*How could I apply this to my life?*

# SECTION 14

Where your heart is stirred the deepest
is where your greatest passion lives.

326. **What I learn after I know it all is what matters.**
*What does this say to me?*

*How could I apply this to my life?*

327. **We lose power when we use power and gain it when we give it.**
*What does this say to me?*

*How could I apply this to my life?*

328. **Questions are actually statements for those who listen for them.**
*What does this say to me?*

*How could I apply this to my life?*

329. **Status quo makes the most sense to the most fearful.**
*What does this say to me?*

*How could I apply this to my life?*

330. **The pain of the struggle reminds us where we need to heal.**
*What does this say to me?*

*How could I apply this to my life?*

331. **The upside of a downward posture is that you're in a position to raise others up.**
*What does this say to me?*

*How could I apply this to my life?*

332. **Humility quickly asks questions, arrogance quickly gives answers.**
*What does this say to me?*

*How could I apply this to my life?*

333. **An inheritance is something I leave to you; a legacy is something I leave in you.**
*What does this say to me?*

*How could I apply this to my life?*

334. **Selfish Talent always loses to Unselfish Character.**
*What does this say to me?*

*How could I apply this to my life?*

335. **Selfishness Divides…Unselfishness Multiplies.**
*What does this say to me?*

*How could I apply this to my life?*

336. **He who is quickest to point out a flaw in another is often saturated by that same flaw himself.**
*What does this say to me?*

*How could I apply this to my life?*

337. **I will chop you down so I look good or build you up so we look good.**
*What does this say to me?*

*How could I apply this to my life?*

338. **It's not about winning, it's about relationships. Winning is temporary, relationships are forever.**
*What does this say to me?*

*How could I apply this to my life?*

**339. Clarifying the WHY behind the WHAT brings about understanding.**

*What does this say to me?*

*How could I apply this to my life?*

**340. Only when I take the time to understand your story can I see the real you.**

*What does this say to me?*

*How could I apply this to my life?*

**341. Fright, Flight or Fight...we choose one of these when adversity hits. We freeze, flee or face it and learn from it.**

*What does this say to me?*

*How could I apply this to my life?*

**342. Point out the potential in others and watch yourself come alive.**

*What does this say to me?*

*How could I apply this to my life?*

**343. Selfishness from one person affects a hundred others.**

*What does this say to me?*

*How could I apply this to my life?*

**344. My daily actions become the words to my life's story.**

*What does this say to me?*

*How could I apply this to my life?*

345. **You eventually become what I expect and believe you can become.**
*What does this say to me?*

*How could I apply this to my life?*

346. **Sharing only part of the truth makes me a liar.**
*What does this say to me?*

*How could I apply this to my life?*

347. **Sometimes it's better to first judge motives than actions.**
*What does this say to me?*

*How could I apply this to my life?*

348. **Where your heart is stirred the deepest is where your greatest passion lives.**
*What does this say to me?*

*How could I apply this to my life?*

349. **A negative thought is a down payment on a mortgage called failure.**
*What does this say to me?*

*How could I apply this to my life?*

350. **Let go of your security and stress will disappear.**
*What does this say to me?*

*How could I apply this to my life?*

# SECTION 15

If expectations are unclear,
accountability is unfair.

351. **You take yourself with you wherever you go. You choose the aroma of roses in your hand or manure on your shoes.**

*What does this say to me?*

*How could I apply this to my life?*

352. **The older I get I will become more and more like I am today. This is either scary or exciting.**

*What does this say to me?*

*How could I apply this to my life?*

353. **Talk about people all day long…as long as it's positives to their face, not negatives behind their back.**

*What does this say to me?*

*How could I apply this to my life?*

354. **Negativity sucks the life out of everything surrounding it.**

*What does this say to me?*

*How could I apply this to my life?*

355. **It's not about who you know, it's knowing a lot about who you know.**

*What does this say to me?*

*How could I apply this to my life?*

356. **Make sure others are buying what you're selling.**

*What does this say to me?*

*How could I apply this to my life?*

357. **Your presence in someone's life makes them feel either anxious and protective or secure and receptive.**

*What does this say to me?*

*How could I apply this to my life?*

358. **Either negative voices from the past or positive choices in the present will determine your future.**

*What does this say to me?*

*How could I apply this to my life?*

359. **When one team member doesn't stand out, the entire team stands out.**

*What does this say to me?*

*How could I apply this to my life?*

360. **Telescopes reveal the big picture…Microscopes reveal the small picture…Stethoscopes reveal the real picture.**

*What does this say to me?*

*How could I apply this to my life?*

361. **A leader's top priority must be to provide clarity.**

*What does this say to me?*

*How could I apply this to my life?*

362. **Having a plan with no deadline is like having a boat with no anchor.**

*What does this say to me?*

*How could I apply this to my life?*

363. **If expectations are unclear, accountability is unfair.**
*What does this say to me?*

*How could I apply this to my life?*

364. **If I'm slow to trust myself, I'll be slow to trust you.**
*What does this say to me?*

*How could I apply this to my life?*

365. **If my enemy is within, my competition has nothing to worry about.**
*What does this say to me?*

*How could I apply this to my life?*

366. **Focus first on what you can do best, not on what the opposition can do to you.**
*What does this say to me?*

*How could I apply this to my life?*

367. **True courage happens when you realize that what you want is worth more than what is standing in your way.**
*What does this say to me?*

*How could I apply this to my life?*

368. **Our most satisfying and sustainable work will happen first within our homes.**
*What does this say to me?*

*How could I apply this to my life?*

369. If a relationship is to stand the test of time, wisdom and discernment say first of all, "go slow."
*What does this say to me?*

*How could I apply this to my life?*

370. Ignoring negative behavior invites more of the same.
*What does this say to me?*

*How could I apply this to my life?*

371. Conflict, Confrontation, Criticism and Correction appear first as cuss words, but can also be very constructive.
*What does this say to me?*

*How could I apply this to my life?*

372. Be slow to hire or promote a person who begs for leadership.
*What does this say to me?*

*How could I apply this to my life?*

373. If you let people know what you stand for, you'll be less likely to fall for the wrong things.
*What does this say to me?*

*How could I apply this to my life?*

374. The biggest mistake I can make is to not admit that I make many of them.
*What does this say to me?*

*How could I apply this to my life?*

**375.** **We did nothing to create ourselves; we weren't even our own idea.**

*What does this say to me?*

*How could I apply this to my life?*

# SECTION 16

If you don't like something, change it;
if you can't change it, don't let it change you

376. **Ask more than you answer.**

*What does this say to me?*

*How could I apply this to my life?*

377. **The more I try to convince you that I'm always right, the more you're convinced that I'm not.**

*What does this say to me?*

*How could I apply this to my life?*

378. **The truth first hurts then heals.**

*What does this say to me?*

*How could I apply this to my life?*

379. **Being head-smart leads to judgment; being heart-smart leads to grace.**

*What does this say to me?*

*How could I apply this to my life?*

380. **If you don't like something, change it; if you can't change it, don't let it change you.**

*What does this say to me?*

*How could I apply this to my life?*

381. **With perspective, release the power to change it and the change itself will power it.**

*What does this say to me?*

*How could I apply this to my life?*

382. **Mechanical problems create windstorms while people problems create hurricanes.**

*What does this say to me?*

*How could I apply this to my life?*

383. **Understand the situation before sharing your solution.**

*What does this say to me?*

*How could I apply this to my life?*

384. **Whether attendance at work or with a kind word, always be on time and even better to be early.**

*What does this say to me?*

*How could I apply this to my life?*

385. **If you don't bring honesty and integrity into a conversation, don't expect to find them when you get there.**

*What does this say to me?*

*How could I apply this to my life?*

386. **We will disappoint people when we do for them what they can do for themselves.**

*What does this say to me?*

*How could I apply this to my life?*

387. **Six powerful words… "I am sorry" and "You were right."**

*What does this say to me?*

*How could I apply this to my life?*

**388.** You know when you're not being honest; acknowledge this privately before others do publicly.

*What does this say to me?*

*How could I apply this to my life?*

**389.** Lack of clear communication results in a lack of trust.

*What does this say to me?*

*How could I apply this to my life?*

**390.** Intentionally focusing every day on what is going right will bring about health, happiness and hope.

*What does this say to me?*

*How could I apply this to my life?*

**391.** The collective personality of the leaders becomes the foundation of the organization.

*What does this say to me?*

*How could I apply this to my life?*

**392.** A parent's love, leadership and influence will be fully displayed in their children's children.

*What does this say to me?*

*How could I apply this to my life?*

**393.** Think like a rookie, act like a veteran.

*What does this say to me?*

*How could I apply this to my life?*

394. **When others succeed in your absence, your leadership is validated and secured.**
*What does this say to me?*

*How could I apply this to my life?*

395. **The closer we are to someone, the greater the chance for conflict and misunderstanding.**
*What does this say to me?*

*How could I apply this to my life?*

396. **The details are the most methodical, time-consuming and necessary part of any endeavor.**
*What does this say to me?*

*How could I apply this to my life?*

397. **The first follower transforms the perceived leader into a believable leader.**
*What does this say to me?*

*How could I apply this to my life?*

398. **Guard your heart when building bigger barns.**
*What does this say to me?*

*How could I apply this to my life?*

399. **Treat internal customers even better than external customers.**
*What does this say to me?*

*How could I apply this to my life?*

**400.** **Above all else, the greatest thing in the entire world is selfless love.**

*What does this say to me?*

*How could I apply this to my life?*